Red Wine
A Glass of Fettle Benefits

A Sip of Boon That Helps You to Stay Fit

Sarwatmika Pal

BLUEROSE PUBLISHERS
India | U.K.

Copyright © Sarwatmika Pal 2024

All rights reserved by author. No part of this publication may be reproduced, stored in a retrieval system or transmitted in any form or by any means, electronic, mechanical, photocopying, recording or otherwise, without the prior permission of the author. Although every precaution has been taken to verify the accuracy of the information contained herein, the publisher assumes no responsibility for any errors or omissions. No liability is assumed for damages that may result from the use of information contained within.

BlueRose Publishers takes no responsibility for any damages, losses, or liabilities that may arise from the use or misuse of the information, products, or services provided in this publication.

For permissions requests or inquiries regarding this publication, please contact:

BLUEROSE PUBLISHERS
www.BlueRoseONE.com
info@bluerosepublishers.com
+91 8882 898 898
+4407342408967

ISBN: 978-93-5989-830-8

Cover design: Sarwatmika Pal
Typesetting: Rohit

First Edition: March 2024

Preface

Red Wine: A Glass of Fettle Benefits is a non-fictional book that delves into red wine consumption that results in an increase in the level of antioxidants. Statistics on the well-being of individual compounds are emerging, but the investigation of red wine itself is restricted. Fettle boon can be demonstrated in epidemiological and animal studies regarding heart diseases, but the information is less firm regarding cancer and nonexistent for other diseases. The evidence cannot be assigned merely to the phytochemical context of wine.

Moderate alcohol intake is known to have satisfaction both physiologically and psychologically. In this mechanism, the phenolic/polyphenolic compound confers benefits that are via their antioxidant activity, intercellular signal modifications, alterations in gene expression, and alteration in microsomal detoxification enzyme activity. On the other hand, the functional modification that occurs due to phenolic/polyphenolic, such as an antimutagenic, anticarcinogenic, or anti-inflammatory activity, is derived from one of these major mechanisms. The handout of red wine to health can only be understood in the context of the whole diet. For populations that consume limited amounts of fruit and vegetables, as in Denmark, the consumption of wine is likely a significant contributing factor for phenolic and other phytochemicals and, consequently, more likely to provide welfare.

In other populations, such as those that consume a Mediterranean-style diet, red wine is less likely to contribute to overall health and disease risk reduction due to the consumption of olive oil, fruits, and vegetables. The recommendation to consume red wine for its beneficial effect may be imprudent due to the health problems that correlate with overuse.

However, if a person drinks alcohol sensibly, red wine has an advantage due to its gratified benefits. There is an age-old argument about what to drink at the end of a long day. Many prefer beer, liquor, and other types of wine. Most don't realize that red wine is the healthiest drink for the client. All over this book will lay hold on a voyage about red wine, first starting with its chronicle, then the facts about why it is healthy in comparison to other alcoholic drinks, and ending up with the overall assertion that red wine is vigorous of alcoholic beverages. As you navigate through the pages of this book, you will discover numerous fascinating facts and elements that may resonate with your own experience, and we are confident that it will strike a chord with its readers. Whether you are a casual reader or an avid book lover, we hope you find something special within the pages of Red Wine: A Glass of Fettle benefits.

The author is passionate and dedicated to writing their thesis and publishing a book on their research. The author expresses about red wine and its fettle boons to all readers that moderate consumption of red wine is good for the health of both men and women. This book is about something other than on account that someone should drink more than one.

Here, the author is in no way condoning heavy alcohol consumption but rather anticipates proving that drinking 1 to 2 glasses a day of red wine can have a positive impact on the buyer's health. In this book, the author expects to prove to the people and convince them that drinking more red wine can have a positive impact on their universal health with the survey the author administrated. The author anticipates confirming her hypothesis that if informed about the health care provision, then people will agree to drink more red wine. The author allotted the survey to about 20 people, and after analysing the results. The author spotted that they manifested her hypothesis with over half of the recipients answering that yes, they would be more inclined to drink red wine.

Red wine is made by using whole grapes, which add vital antioxidants and vitamins to the human system. Again, to be clear, the author is not advocating that people drink more alcohol. After being properly informed by a credible source of its various health benefits. Red wine contains a polyphenol called resveratrol, which has various cardiovascular benefits as well as other helpful attributes. Doctors apprise that excessive alcohol consumption can lead to serious health problems. Instead, I am proving that when choosing to drink, it would be in a person's best interest to choose red wine because it is the healthiest alcohol for someone to consume. So, remember, after a long, tiring day, a glass of red wine might be what the doctor ordered.

Acknowledgement

The world is a better place thanks to people who want to develop and lead others. What makes it even better are people who share the gift of their time to mentor future leaders. Thank you to everyone who strives for me to grow and help others grow. It is the business version of Red wine, a glass of fettle benefits. To all the individuals I have the opportunity to lead, be led by, or watch their leadership from afar, thank you for being the inspiration and foundation for The Leadership Manifesto.

This book exists because of the experiences and support from my parents and the team of Blue Rose publishers at Ultimate Software. You have given me the opportunity to lead a great group of individuals—to be a leader of great leaders is a blessed place to be. Thank you to Dr Desh Deepak Pal, Nidhi Srivastav and Prapti Gupta

Having an idea and turning it into a book is as hard as it sounds. The experience is both internally challenging and rewarding. I especially want to thank the individuals who helped make this happen. Thanks to all my brothers, mother, and sisters for their unwavering guidance.

Overview of book

The book **Red Wine: A Glass of Fettle Benefits** is written by author **Sarwatmika Pal** to the attention of all readers towards the health benefits of red wine, the origin of red wine, how it is processed, red wine is a lifestyle, data analysis conclusion and result, types of red wine and comparison as this book is non-fictional. The author is a college student who loves to research and write a book according to the experiences and systematic analysis of any topic regarding the subject, as we all learn from our experiences and attain knowledge.

This book consists of 5 chapters that describe red wine in depth.

In Chapter 1, the author introduces red wine, namely resveratrol, which has numerous health benefits that will be further explained in detail in this book. Wine is frequently quoted in the bible from Nora and his grapevine to Jesus as wine is a catholic church as an alternative for the blood of Christ, which is an indication of the crucial role that beverage has played in years past. Experts agree that the wine dates from 6000 BC. Wine was made in Egypt and in Mesopotamia, Greece, Spain, Mexico, Rome, and the United States. Spain played a major role in winemaking. Red wine is known as the healthiest alcohol due to the fermentation and production process, as it contains antioxidant vitamins and polyphenols.

In chapter 2, the author expresses the fettle benefits of red wine that prevent heart disease. Red wine lowers bad cholesterol. Researches show that alcohol in red wine increases good cholesterol (HDL) by about 5-15%. Red wine keeps your body slim. It boosts brain health. The antioxidant could also provide a higher energy level. One glass of wine per day for females and 2 glasses of wine for males is sufficient. In this chapter, red wine is compared with other beverages like red wine vs white wine, Red wine vs beer and Red wine vs vodka. Red wine contains 125 calories per glass, while white wine contains 115 calories per glass. Red wine prevents sunburn, while beer acts as a vitamin booster. Red wine consists of 99mg of potassium, while vodka contains 1 mg of potassium in it.

In Chapter 3, the author describes how red wine is processed in a scientific way. Firstly, grapes are harvested, and then grapes are prepared for adding yeast. After that, the fermentation process occurs, and grapes are pressed so that their juice may come out. After that, the chemical process known as Malolactic fermentation occurs when bacteria convert sharp malic acid into smoother inside the tank. Then, red wine is aged in barrels for several months to a year in oak barrels to enhance red wine with aromatic compounds. After that, the winemaker blends grape varieties or barrels together to create the final wine. Then, clarification of bottling and the bottle ageing process occurs.

In Chapter 4, you will study the fermentation of red wine kept for 21 days and other observations like hedonic scale ranking test sensitivity test numerical score, composite score with thesis questionnaire and result as the author took 20 people under observation for its quality.

Chapter 5 consist of types of red wine like Shiraz Melbec, Merlot, Mish Zinfandel Barbera, and Cabernet Sauvignon, with the conclusion of red wine. The author justifies the title of the book through her skills of analysis and explanation. The book is written in a friendly tone, with pictures for each chapter. If a reader carefully analyses each picture for each chapter, then he/she can relate the content of the chapters to the pictures. A person who loves to read deeply into any topic would love the book. However, the language used in the book is simple to understand. The book has so many pictures for each section that a reader may get immersed and ultimately need to remember the significance of the section.

Contents

1. How is Red Wine innovated? 1
2. Cheers to Good Health! 9
3. How Red Wine is Manufactured? 19
4. Data Analysis of Red Wine 25
5. Famous Red Wine around the world 43

CHAPTER ONE

How is Red Wine innovated?

Introduction

Red wine is popular worldwide, and it is beneficial for health due to the amount of compound present in it. Red wine is the healthiest alcohol due to its fermentation and production process, as it contains significantly more antioxidants, vitamins and polyphenols than most other available alcohols. The tradition of winemaking and wine consumption has been known for many centuries as the ancient Romans knew the health benefits of wine, and they made it popularised all over the world. The key component of red wine is resveratrol, which is the most important polyphenol in red wine as it contains Anthocyanin, Catechins and Tanis (Proanthocyanin and Ellagitannin), and it aids the bodily system. Since much available research and numerous studies were conducted, they proved that resveratrol improves the cardiovascular system and has an impact on decreasing the risk of obesity and two types of diabetes.

It contains cardioprotective effects that improve endothelial function and glucose metabolism, reducing inflammation and regulating blood lipids. Resveratrol has numerous health benefits that will be explained further in detail in the fettle benefits section of this book, while the most far-famed seminar of wine compound upstream is polyphenol. The headstone component of polyphenol composition and in-depth content is a variety of grapes. White wine contains less polyphenol than red wine. The total polyphenolic content in white wine is in terms of 100 mg GAEL[1] (Gallic acid equivalent), whereas red wine contains thousands of mg GAEL[1] of total polyphenols. In order to prove the hypothesis, people will drink more red wine if properly edified of its kilter boon, as further research has been done.

The survey was to be conducted where various questionnaires regarding current drinking habits and preferences, along with prior knowledge of red wine, were catechized. The last questionnaire were aimed to prove the hypothesis by first notifying the respondents of the many health effects of red wine and then asking if they would be more willing to drink red wine after knowing its benefits for the body. This book will systematically inform the reader about the literature on red wine, processing and fermentation of red wine, observations, data analysis of processed wine, health benefits of red wine, type of red wine and analysis of the survey result. The tip is to convince the reader to drink red wine versus other alcohol forms.

Origin of red wine

Wine is an alcoholic beverage that has been popular for mankind for thousands of years. Wine is typically made from fermented grape juice. Yeast consumes sugar in grapes, and then it is converted into ethanol, carbon dioxide and heat. Different varieties of grapes and strains of yeast produce different styles of wine. Wine is frequently quoted in the Bible from Nora and his grapevine to Jesus. Wine is used in the Catholic Church as an alternative to the blood of Christ, which is an indication of the crucial role that beverage has played in years past. It is often said that Western society constructs its foundation on wine. Many centuries ago, the wine industry was a sign of a provident country as a developed society could build an affluent and competitive wine industry. Winemaking and drinking have a long history. Experts agree that wine dates from

6000 BC. Wine was made in Egypt and in Mesopotamia, Greece, Spain, Mexico, Rome and the United States. Spain plays a major role in the winemaking process.

The premature production of red wine began in 6000 BC in Georgia (a region between Europe and Asia). Red wine cultivation was first laid by Egyptians, and they were sketched on the walls of their religious temple. Firstly, grapes were harvested by using a curved knife. Then they were set down in a Wicker basket, and then they were placed in vats of acacia wood, and then they were tramped until they got liquefied. It is believed that red wine was discovered unexpectedly by a farmer there storing grapes, and they may have left some leftover grapes in the barrel. The leaving of grapes in the barrel caused fermentation, and hence, wine was produced. The first known vineyard was discovered around 4100 BC in a cave in Armenia (coffee 2011). Red wine is classified into six main varieties of red grapes, namely:-

Cabernet Sauvignon

It is the youngest red wine, although it is less than 600 years old. Sauvignon grapes were first mentioned in the 18th century and are known as hard wine in French. This is a popular wine that is cultivated in Australia and that yields a rich and ripe flavour. Flavour - Bell pepper, herbs, green olives and black cherry black.

Chianti

This is known as Italian wine, and it dates back to the 15th century. The tasting of Chianti is characterized by red and black cherry characters, along with savoury notes, wild herbs and spice, supported by racy acidity and well-structured tannins. Chianti's winemaking zone is located between the cities of Florence (to the north) and Siena (to the south) and stretches into these provinces plus Prato, Arezzo, Pistoia and Pisa.

The main type of grape used in Sangiovese grapes to yield luscious wine is Berry fruitiness.

Merlot

It is known as one of the oldest wines in France, dating back to the first century.

It is cultivated in the Bordeaux region of France, and it is difficult to grow them due to their large size and thin skin. It is frequently called Chardonnay of reds as it is easy to pronounce.

It ripens decently and forms plump and wonderful wines that may age for decades.

Flavour: Watermelon, Strawberry, Cherry and Plum.

Sangiovese

These grapes were used in Tuscany in 1722, and they are grown there today. They are used in the production of Chianti wines. It is light in colour and dynamically acidic.

Flavour: Pie, Cherry, Tobacco leaf.

Zinfandel

These grapes are known as the oldest variety of grapes that are pre-owned and flourished in California as they came about in the 1830s. Its extraction has been traced to Croatia.

Flavour: Raspberry, Blackberry, Black cherry, Raisin prunes.

CHAPTER TWO

Cheers to Good Health!

Health benefits of Red Wine

Red wine is an ambiguous blade all over the world for health and wellness as alcohol typically has a negative impact on overall health; the skin and seed of red grapes contain certain antioxidants like flavonoid resveratrol that cause scale back unfettle LDL cholesterol levels, the growth rate of HDL cholesterol level, cease multiplication of certain cancerous tumour and upgrade the health of neuron. According to the testimony of recent studies, globbing red wine daily can have a positive impact on consumers' health. The clue sponsor in red wine is polyphenol resveratrol, as polyphenol is an antioxidant that is present in many foods like legumes, pomegranates, cranberries, cherries, blueberries, honey grapes, and green tea. Polyphenols have anti-cancer properties and reduce coronary artery disease (Scarlbert, 2005). Polyphenols are a group of chemical substances that are present in plants and other foods like red grapes. Flavonoid is the most abundant polyphenol that is present in the classic diet. Red wine contains tannins. Tannis contain flavonoid polyphenol. Many researchers found that some of the polyphenols present in red wine help prevent cardiovascular disease and certain cancers. Flavonoids consist of polymer chains that are made of proanthocyanidins or OPs.

OPCS is found in numerous types of plants, grapes, seeds and skin. OPCS consist of various types of benefits for venous and capillary disorders, venous insufficiency, capillary fragility, diabetic retinopathy, and macular degeneration. The impact of OPCDs includes neutralizing oxidant free radicals, lowering blood fat and inhibiting collagen breakdown. OPCs help to prevent cardiovascular disease by diminishing the negative effects of high-ranking cholesterol present in the heart and blood vessels. OPCs, usually up to 1 gram per litre, are present in red wine. Resveratrol is present in the skin of red grapes, which are also known as vine grapes, which are cultivated in cooler climates and have higher levels of resveratrol than in weather. Malbec, Sirah pinot, and noir types of grapes have the thickest epicarp and high levels of resveratrol. Resveratrol prevents damage to blood vessels, reduces low-density lipoproteins (LDL) cholesterol and prevents clotting blood. Red wine has its benefits, namely: -

1. Prevent heart diseases.

2. Research reveals that people who drink 150 ml of red wine per day may have a 32% lowered chance of heart disease.

3. Red wine is lower in bad cholesterol. Research shows that alcohol in red wine increases good cholesterol (HDL) by about 5-15%, whereas non-alcoholic red wine alters their boon and gains LDL levels.

4. Reduce the risk of cancer.

5. Control blood sugar levels. Some studies show that women who drink red wine in moderate amounts experience low diabetic readings as compared to men.

6. Keep your body slime.

7. Keep memory sharp as resveratrol present in red wine blocks the formation of beta-amyloid protein, a key ingredient in the plaque of the brain of people with Alzheimer's.

8. The risk of depression.

9. Many studies carried out that middle-aged to older adults should drink a moderate amount of red wine daily so as to keep depression away.

10. Positive effect on the digestive system.

11. Due to its antibacterial nature, red wine has treated stomach irritation and cured other digestive disorders as it has been proven to reduce the risk of infections by Helicobacter pylori, a bacterium that is found in the stomach.

Red Wine is Life Style !

Red wine is good for health as it is rich in antioxidants, which may vary in taste and colour. That is prepared by crushing and fermenting dark-coloured grapes.

There are many varieties of red wine, namely Merlot, Pinot Noir and Shiraz. Red wine is known for joy, happiness, sorrow, health and Good memories with vibes as it adorns your inner world.

Antioxidants reduce oxidative stress in the body. Oxidative stress has clear links with many diseases, including cancers and heart disease.

There are many healthful, antioxidant-rich foods, including fruits, nuts, and vegetables.

According to the [American Heart Association (AHA)](#), resveratrol — an antioxidant in red wine — may reduce [blood pressure](#) and increase levels of HDL (good) cholesterol.

To stay safe, people should stay within official CDC guidelines from the Centers for Disease and Prevention (CDC) Trusted Source, which define moderate drinking as:

- 1 glass of wine per day for females
- 2 glasses of wine for males

One glass of wine is 5 ounces (oz) of 12% alcohol by volume.

According to the American Diabetes Association, drinking red wine can lower your blood sugar for up to 24 hours. However, aside from that, there is some research that shows how red wine can help people with diabetes. Research done by French scientists reveals that resveratrol in red wine can increase lifespan by as much as 60%

The antioxidants could also provide higher energy levels. Though the tests have been conducted on worms, researchers believe similar effects can be seen in humans. Resveratrol might activate an evolutionary stress response in human cells that might enhance longevity.

An Italian study says that wine can increase lifespan by inducing longevity genes. According to the Stanford Center on Longevity, resveratrol in red wine can protect our neurons from the undesirable effects of ageing.

Red wine has many benefits, namely –

- It Boost Brain Health
- Promotes Liver Health
- Improves Bone Strength
- Fight Depression
- Improves Sleep

- Tooth Decay
- Slow Down Aging and Makes Skin Glow
- Keeps You Slim
- Regulate Blood Sugar
- Keep Heart Healthy
- Reduce the Risk of Cancer

"A Good Book , A Good Wine , Makes a Good Life" !

Red Wine offers a long life!

One study found that middle-aged Italian men who drank up to five glasses of wine a day— almost all of it red—tended to live longer than men who drank more or less alcohol.

Moderate wine consumption is a characteristic of the Mediterranean diet. Studies around the world have shown a beneficial effect of moderate alcohol intake, especially wine, on health. It was first described by Ancel Keys in the Seven Countries study.

Moderate alcohol consumption, especially wine, is generally regarded to be beneficial to health.

Moderate wine intake, at 1–2 glasses per day as part of the Mediterranean diet, has been positively associated with human health promotion, disease prevention, and disease prognosis.

The beneficial role of red wine has been attributed to its phytochemical compounds, as highlighted by clinical trials, where the effect of red wine has been compared to white wine, non-alcoholic wine, other alcoholic drinks, and water.

The most recent studies confirm the valuable role of moderate wine consumption, especially red wine, in the prevention and treatment of chronic diseases such as cardiovascular disease, metabolic syndrome, cognitive decline, depression, and cancer. Additionally, binge drinking and high alcohol intake have also been associated with negative health impacts.

"A glass of wine is good for health and the leftover is good for your morale"

Comparison with other alcohols

The benefit of red wine compared to three other commonly consumed drinks: white wine, beer, and Vodka. While all alcoholic drinks, consumed in moderation, possess some beneficial qualities.

Red wine has the most abundant qualities and is the best choice for consumers in comparison to this other alcoholic beverage.

Red wine is least harmful to consumers, frequently has the most antioxidants available, and contains the most beneficial polyphenols for affecting the human body.

Red Wine vs White wine

Red wine contains resveratrol, and white wine contains tyrosol and hydroxytyrosol. These two antioxidants, in comparison to resveratrol, only provide minor artery blockage.

They are not as strong as resveratrol, and they are not rich in antioxidants. While resveratrol is more commonly found in food, namely berries, grapes, and legumes, tyrosol and hydroxytyrosol are commonly found in oils, particularly in olive oil.

The fermentation process for red wine includes using the grape's skin. The grape's skin contains the most antioxidants and vitamins, which are higher levels than white wines because the skin isn't used in the fermentation process for white wine; it decreases its overall medical benefits.

White wine is also not an adequate source of resveratrol. Facts show that white wine also contains more sugar in calories than red wine.

Red wine vs beer

In comparison to resveratrol in red wine, beer contains hops, yeast and grain. These all contain high levels of carbohydrates, a small amount of B vitamins, and Potassium.

Drinking beer in excess can increase the risk of liver cancer, cirrhosis, alcoholism, and obesity, and beer is the most prone to drink.

There is also a phenomenon called beer. Beer bellies are brought by consuming too many calories. Beer bellies increase the amount of strain placed on the heart and joints.

Beer is considered liquid calories, meaning it offers no sense of fullness, and an average of 150 calories are consumed when drinking one beer. These calories can lead to a multitude of problems with weight and blood pressure into two types of diabetes. Beer makes you hungry.

Overconsumption is prominent when people consume beer, and long-term use can lead to malnutrition, memory loss, mental problems, heart problems, and an increase in blood pressure. The Mayo Clinic has data on occasional reports of asthma being triggered due to beer consumption. Drinking beer increases blood fats called triggered, and when in large, these can lead to arterial blockage. Drinking beer provides the strongest hangover, and beer has been proven to slow down the CNS. It is recommended for a patient undergoing surgery to quit drinking beer before the procedure in order to protect against showing off their CNS.

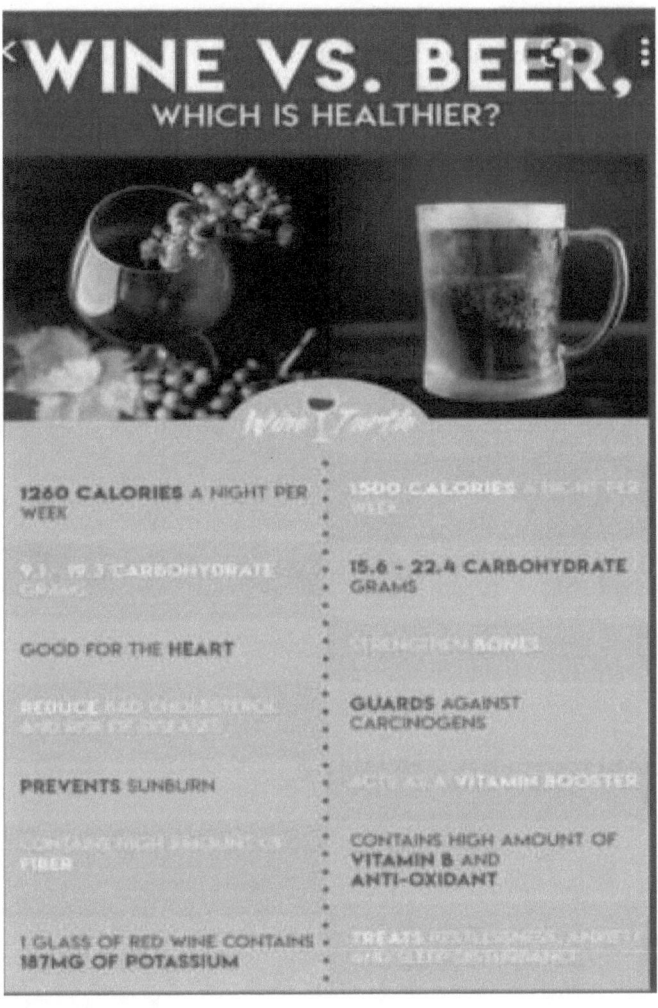

Red wine vs Vodka

Vodka, much like beer, is commonly abused and is one of the main alcohols that cause addiction. Vodka causes intoxication easily and quickly.

Made with potatoes, not grapes, Vodka contains little to no antioxidant value and no resveratrol.

Some health effects from drinking vodka include heart disease, cancer, and brain damage, and it can also cause negative effects on sleep.

Processing of red wine

CHAPTER THREE

How Red Wine is Manufactured?

Methodology

Ingredients

- Grapes - 3kg
- Sugar - 1.5 kg
- Long Pepper - 4 pieces
- Cinnamon - 4 sticks
- Cardamom - 4 pieces
- Cloves - 4 piece
- Crushed ginger – Small piece
- Tulsi powder dried in sunlight – 3 table spoon.
- Lemon water (4 tablespoon)
- (Apple 1/2 and orange juice1/2)
- Beet roots – 200 grms
- Yeast – 40 capsules
- Wheat crushed - 200grms

Equipment's for Red wine

Churning Rod Wooden

Ceramic Jar

Siever

Binding Cloth

Grinder (For Wheat)

Mixer (For Apple and Oranges juice)

Bowl (For activation of yeast)

Cotton Cloth

Storing Jars (Glass)

Vessel for Washing Grapes

Cork Bottles

Sterilized Wine Bottles Stainless Steel Grater

Processing of Red wine (within 21 days)

Part -1

- Use boiled and cooling water only
- Take 3kg of Grapes
- Wash the grapes in boiled and cooled water
- Remove all the stems
- Pat it dry
- After drying fill it in Ceramic jar
- Use a wooden Churning rod for mashing grapes
- Take 1.5 KG of sugar

- Mash the batter until the sugar starts to melt
- Take long pepper 4 pieces and add in it
- Add cinnamon sticks – 4 pieces
- Add cardamom – 4 pieces
- Add cloves – 4 pieces
- Crushed ginger - small piece
- Add Tulsi powder – 3 tablespoon
- Add 4 tablespoon lemon water and half apple half orange juice
- For color red add beetroot 200 gram
- Boil beetroot for two to three minutes
- Drain and store water
- Add beetroot juice in ceramic jar
- Wheat slightly crushed 200 grams
- Mix it well
- Lukewarm water add one tablespoon yeast
- Sugar one tablespoon
- Keep it for few minutes for activation of yeast
- Add yeast in ceramic jar
- Don't close lid tightly
- Cover and tie it with a cloth
- Stir after 24 hours with a wooden spoon for 21days

Processing of wine

(Part 2)

1. On 21th day today open the batter and mix it well
2. Use sterilized vessel and bottle
3. Strain the liquid and keep it in a jar or bottle
4. Run the wine into the bottles
5. Leave half inch space of for cork

FLOW DIAGRAM FOR RED WINE MAKING

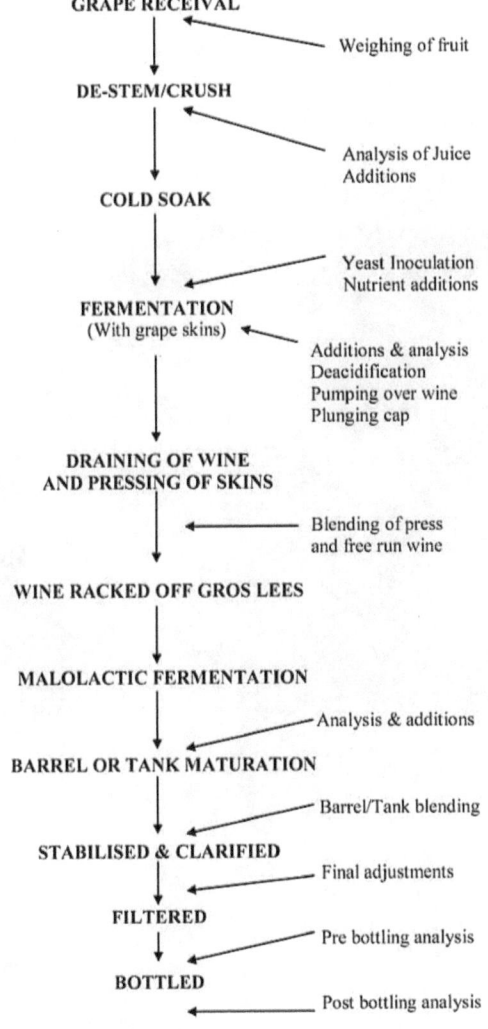

CHAPTER FOUR

Data Analysis of Red Wine

Fermentation of Red Wine

Observation of wine (21day)

Date	Temperature Normal temperature (20-30*C)	Humidity Normal humidity (50-70%)	Temperature fluctuation (20-30*C)
27 Feb	25*C	31%	No change
28 Feb	28*C	32 %	No change
1 March	22*C	32 %	25*C
2 March	28*C	35 %	Constant
3 March	28*C	31 %	Constant
4 March	26*C	30 %	Constant
5 March	30*C	32 %	Constant
6 March	20*C	67 %	No change

7 March	30*C	35 %	No change
8 March	26*C	32 %	No change
9 March	29*C	43%	30*C
10 March	29*C	43 %	No change
11 March	30*C	29 %	28*C
12 March	21*C	32 %	25*C
13 March	30*C	42 %	No change
14 March	30*C	47 %	26*C
15 March	22*C	42 %	No change
16 March	26*C	57 %	20 – 30 *C
17 March	25*C	60 %	No change
18 March	30*C	57 %	28*C
19 March	25*C	73 %	No change

Observation Scale

Hedonic Scale	Ranking Test	Sensitive Test	Numerical Scoring	Composite Score Test
Like extremely- 9	1st Rank	Weak – 1	Excellent 90%	Quality 20
Like very much – 8	2nd Rank	Medium – 2	Good 80%	Color 20
Like moderate – 7	3rd Rank	Strong – 3	Fair 70%	Consistency 20
Like slightly – 6	4th Rank	Very Strong-4	Poor 60%	Flavor 40
Neither like or dislike -5		Extremely strong -5		Absence of defect – 20
Dislike slightly – 4				
Dislike moderately- 3				
Dislike very much - 2				
Dislike extremely - 1				

In following observation and data representation –

- Statistical representation (Bar graph, Pie chart)

- No consumer kept under observation = 20 people.
  Formula = Total no of consumer satisfied/20

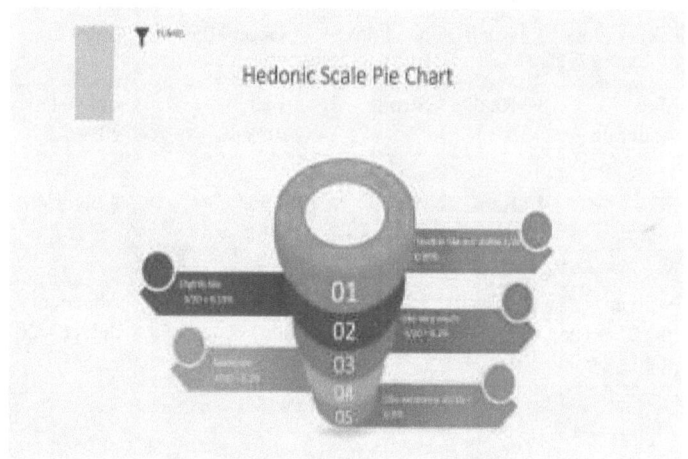

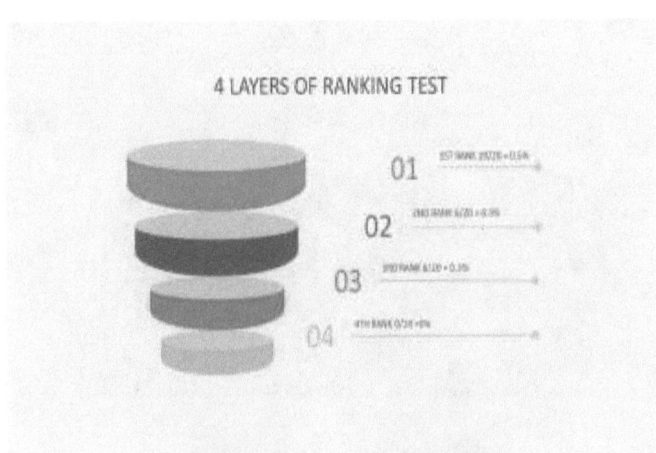
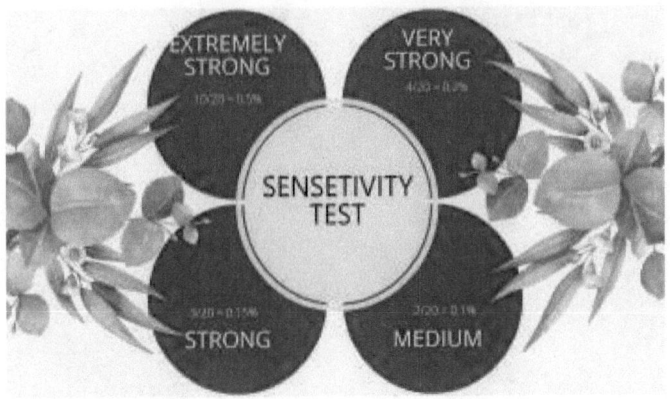

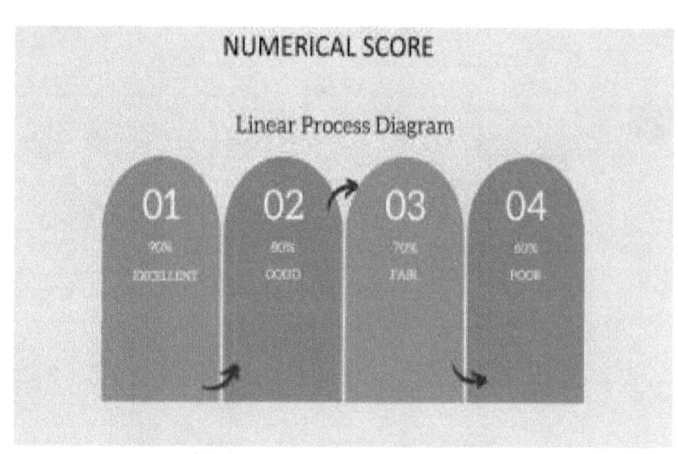

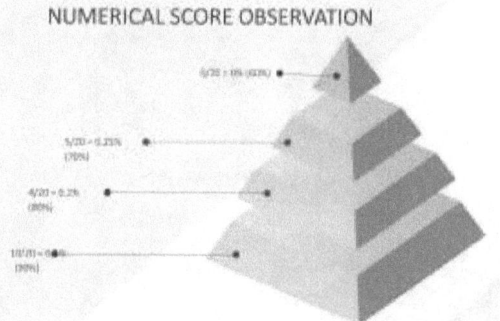

COMPOSITE SCORE CHART

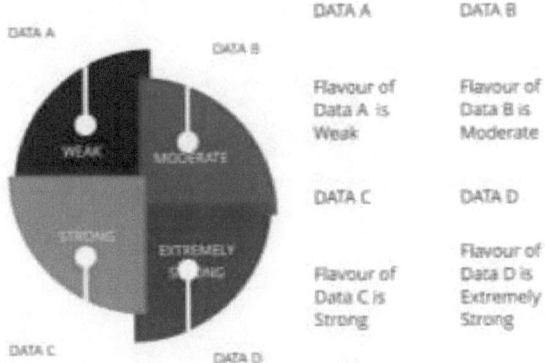

DATA A

Flavour of Data A is Weak

DATA B

Flavour of Data B is Moderate

DATA C

Flavour of Data C is Strong

DATA D

Flavour of Data D is Extremely Strong

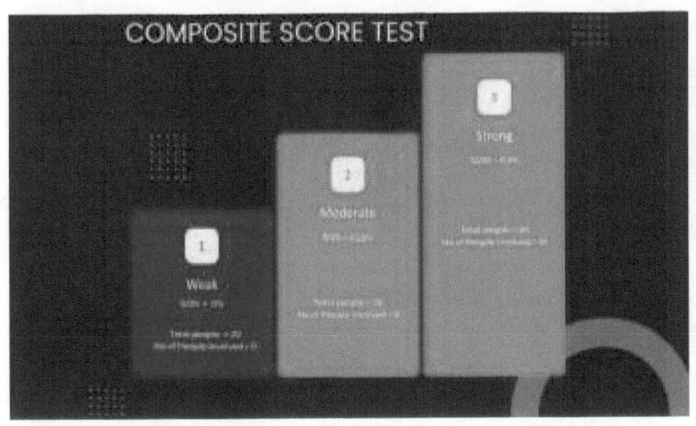

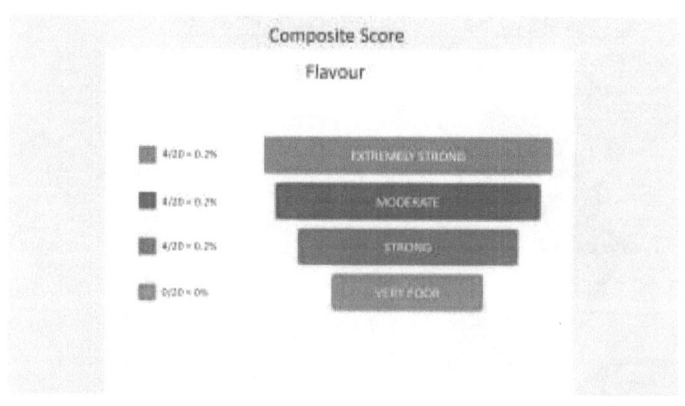

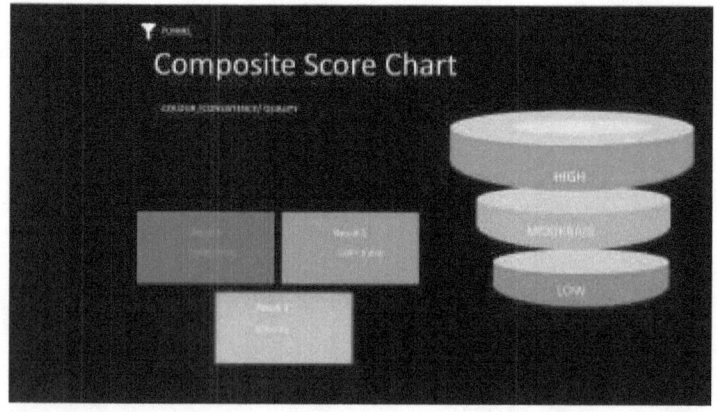

Appendix

Examination

How is the taste flavour odour of red wine?

   a) Excellent

   b) Good

   c) Moderate

   d) Sightly like

   e) Poor

How is the colour of red wine?

    a) Extremely strong

    b) Strong

    c) Very strong

    d) Moderate

    e) Weak

What rank will you give to red wine?

    a) 1st Rank

    b) 2nd Rank

    c) 3rd Rank

    d) 4th Rank

What is the numerical score of red wine?

    a) 90%

    b) 80%

    c) 70%

    d) 60%

How is the quality of red wine?

    a) A grade

    b) B grade

    c) C grade

    d) D grade

Is there any defect in this product?

a) Yes

b) No

Do you like to drink red wine?

a) Yes

b) No

After reading this excerpt about red wine will you drink wine?

Antioxidant in red wine called polyphenol helps to protect the linning of blood vessel in your heart. A polyphenol called resvetrol is one substance in red wine that is present in it. Resvetrol be a key ingredient in red wine that helps to prevent damage to blood vessel and reduces LDL cholesterol and prevent blood clot

a) Yes

b) No

Result

At The End of My Thesis, I Hereby That From the Above Observations, Data, Statistical Representation of Red Wine (Bar Graph), Pie Charts, Hedonic Scale, Ranking Test, Sensitivity Test, Numerical Scoring, Composite Score, and other Mathematical Calculations Resembles That The Flavour,

Odour, Taste, Colour, Texture and Consistency of Red Wine Is Meritorious as The Backbone (Methodology) of My Clock in Hypothesis Interpreted That It Depends on The Way You Processed Your Red Wine Is It Processed in Organic or

Inorganic Way and Did You Work In Organizing or NonOrganizing Manner (Step by Step According To Its Methodology) as It Lean on Certain Factors That Should be Kept In Mind. Dispose of Red Wine Factors PH, Temperature,

Humidity, Vibration, Light, Temperature Change, Refrigeration, Cold Storage Place, Oxygen Removal and Many Intrinsic and Extrinsic Factors Are Responsible for the Colour, Taste, Flavour, Odour, And Consistency of Red Wine. If There Is Fluctuation in Both Intrinsic and Extrinsic Factors, Then It

Will Cause an Impact on Its Colour, Flavour, Texture, and Odour, and It Causes Many Changes in the Quality of Red Wine as well.

PH Also Play an Important Role in Changes in the Colour, Flavour, Odour and Texture of Red Wine. Throughout My-Ongoing research, I Took 20 People and Their Observations and summarised many Questionnaires Regarding Taste, Colour, Odour, Texture and Quality. Many People Gave Their Positive Impact on Its Taste, Odour, Colour and Quality. They Apprise Me That Its Quality Is Strong as It Can Be Sold to Wine Shops in the Market, and They Even Reveal That There Is No Defect in Red Wine's Colour, Odour, Texture and Flavour. This book also conveys to people the Health Benefits of Red Wine and creates awareness of Its Benefits among people So That They Can Consume More Red Wine in smaller Amounts. If You Like Drinking Red Wine, There Is No Need to Worry Unless You

Exceed the Recommended Amount, as In Europe and America, Moderate Red Wine Consumption Is Considered to Be 1-1.5 Glasses a Day for Women and 1-2 Glasses a Day for Men as Many Studies Showed That 1-3 Glass of Red Wine per day, 34 days of Week May Reduce Risk of Stroke in Middle Aged Man.

Chapter 5   Types of Red Wine

CHAPTER FIVE

Famous Red Wine around the world

Types of red wine

After being informed the reader about the health benefits of red wine, it is deemed necessary to provide the reader with the eight best red wines for consumers. Below are the top eight best red wines for consumers as ranked by the amount of resveratrol flavour antioxidant and ability to be paired with food.

Shiraz (syrah)

This type of wine is grown in California, Australia and Rhone Valley in France. This type of wine typically has the aroma and flavour of wild black fruit with an overtone of black pepper spices and roaster meat.

The Shiraz variety produces hearty, spicey red, and it gives some of the world's finest, deepest, and darkest red wine with intense flavour and phenomenal longevity.

This is one red wine that absolutely must be served at room temperature or warm because of the abundance of flavour. It is best paired with meat such as steak and beef.

Syrah wine has a rich flavour, smooth tannins, and an alcohol content of up to 15%

Shiraz grapes are cultivated around the world and have one of the highest antioxidant contents of any red wine for health purposes.

Pinot Noir

This type of red wine is grown in Australia, California, Oregon, and New Zealand. Pinot noir is considered to be the noblest red wine because it is difficult to grow, rarely blended, and produces no roughness.

The taste structure of this wine is delicate and fresh. Its flavour is like cherry strawberry plum and often has an aroma that smells like tea leaves, damp earth, or worn leather. Pinot noir is best paired with food like grilled salmon chicken and Japanese dishes.

Merlot

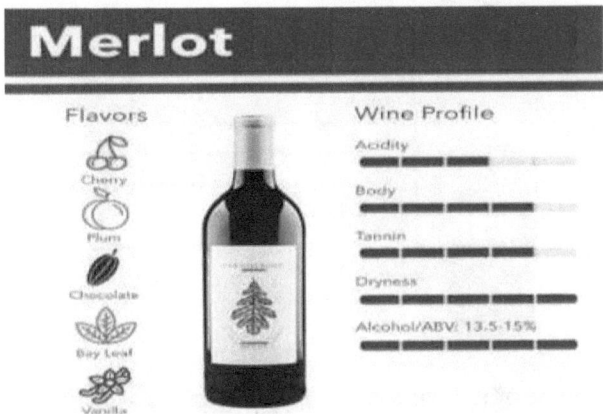

This wine is the easiest red wine to drink. It has a softness about it that has made it an introducing wine for new red wine drinkers.

Merlot is a key part of the Bordeaux blend, and it is mainly grown in Italy, Romania, California, Washington State, Chile, and Australia. These grapes produce a taste similar to that of black cherry, plum and other herbal flavours.

The texture is round, and the Merlot type of wine is less tannic or rough than most other types of red wine. Fortunately, this versatile type of red wine can be paired with any food. Merlot is mixed with cabernet for flavour.

Cabernet Sauvignon

This type of red wine is typically accepted as one of the world's best varieties. It undergoes a rigorous oak treatment that causes it to be blended with cabernet franc and merlot. It is planted wherever red wine grapes are grown except in extreme northern fringes such as Germany.

It is predominantly grown in places like Australia, Chile, and California. Cabernet Sauvignon is a full-bodied wine with a firm and gripping taste when it is younger. This means that, at first, it will have a current taste but will fade away to that of a bell pepper. This type of red wine is best paired with prepared red meat.

Malbec

This type of wine was born in the French Bordeaux region, but now it is widely grown in Argentina, where it is the most prominent type of red wine.

It is also grown in Chile, Australia, and in the cooler region of California. Malbec is a trickier type of wine because its taste and characteristics depend greatly on where it is grown and from where its fermentation process goes. Usually, it produces a well-coloured red wine that tastes like berries, plums, and spice. This red wine can be paired with all types of meat-based meals like Mexican Cajun and Indian-style dishes.

Zinfandel

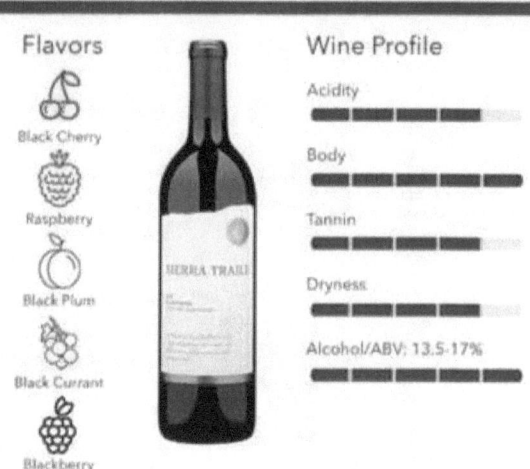

This grape is one of the world's most versatile because it makes everything from white to blush to rich and heavy red wine.

These grapes are only found in California and often have a zesty flavour of berry and pepper, and they are best paired with tomato sauce, pasta pizza, and grilled barbecued meat. This type of wine is produced in Italy, the Tuscany region, and parts of California.

It typically tastes like fresh plums and berries, and it is best paired with Italian and Mediterranean-style food.

Barbera

It typically tastes like fresh plums and berries, and it is best paired with Italian and Mediterranean-style food.

Barbera, this type of red wine, is a classic wine of Italian origin and is now grown widely in California. It tastes like juice, black cherries, and plum fruit, and it has a silky texture with excellent acidity.

Barbera red wine is also very versatile and can be paired with many dishes, especially those that include tomato sauce.

Mish

Mash flavour: The taste of Barbera has notes of strawberry and sour cherry flavours that are synonymous with light-bodied wines. Light tannins and high acidity make it taste juicy.

The red wine with the healthiest benefits is one that contains malbec and Madeiran grapes because of their level of OPC's.

In order to be labelled as these specific types of wine, they must contain at least 40% or more resveratrol. The other varieties that are high in resveratrol level are Petite, Shirah, St Laurent and Pinot Noir.

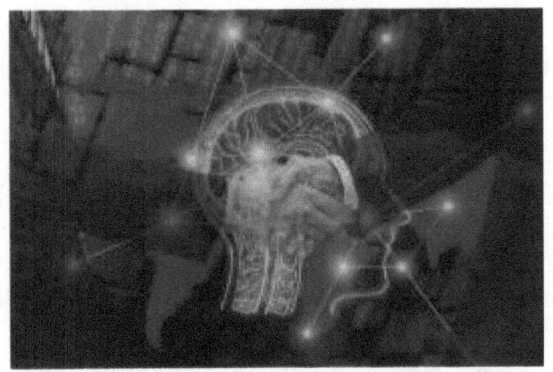

Conclusion

Red Wine Is Not Only the Best Wine for Consumers but Also the Best Alcohol Overall. Based on The Amount of antioxidants present and The Amount of Resveratrol in Red Wine, It Is Proven To Be The Healthiest and Most Beneficial Alcohol for Consumers. One of The Key Takeaway and Key Factors That Make Red Wine More Beneficial Than Other
Forms of Alcohol, Especially White Wine, Is During Its Production and Fermentation Process, the Grapes are used. The Skin of Any

Fruit Is Abundant in Antioxidants and Vitamins, and More Often Than Not, the Skin Contains More antioxidants than the Actual Meat of Fruit because Red Wine Is Made with The Skin of Red Grapes.

It automatically has more antioxidant vitamins and polyphenols than white wine. The Main Reason Behind This Is Why Red Wine Is Healthy Because of Resveratrol. Resveratrol Has an Abundance of Wonderful Health Effects Ranging from Cardiovascular Improvement to Lowering Risk for Two Types of Diabetes for Helping Ease Depression. Not Coincidently, Though, Most Resvetrol Is Contained in the Skin of Red Grapes. So, If Red Wine Wasn't Made Using Skin, It Most Likely Wouldn't have Nearly as Many Good Attributes as It Does. The Main Problem with Red Wine Is That Consumers Aren't Aware of Its Many Useful Health Effects. Stores don't Do a Good Job of Advertising It, and Neither Do Other Forms of Advertisement.

Even Walking into The Liquor Store and Asking a Clerk About the Health Effects of Red Wine Proved Useless, Seeing a Clerk Not Knowledgeable About Red Wine's Many Benefits. The Survey Results Proved That If Properly Informed About the Health Benefits of Red Wine, Consumers Are More Likely to Drink It. Fortunately, Enough People Already Drink Red Wine because They Like It, So Even Though They May Have Been Unaware of Its Benefits, they are still Making Their Bodies feel good. However, Some of The Survey Results Showed That People Who Did Not Drink Red Wine Would be Inclined to Drink It After Learning About It Multiple Beneficial Health Effects. This Paper Is Not Advocating for More Alcohol Consumption. If Anything, It's Advocating for Proper Alcohol Consumption.

Consuming Excessive Amounts of Alcohol Is Extremely Detrimental to a Person's Health. The Point of This Paper Was to Show That When Choosing to Drink, It Would be in the best interest to Choose to Drink Red Wine at The End of a Long Day 1/2. Glasses

of Red Wine Will Help Rejuvenate Your Senses. The Abundance of antioxidants and vitamins, as well as The Resveratrol in Red Wine, Will Add Something of Value to Someone's Immune System. More Research Needs To be Done to Further Validate the Positive Effects of Resveratrol on The
Human Body, But There Is No Doubt That When Choosing Something to Drink, The Consumer Should Choose Red Wine because It Is the Best and Healthiest Alcohol Available for Consumption.

Referance

Lukas P. Inventing Wine: A New History of One of the World's Most Ancient Pleasures. WW Norton & Company; New York,

NY, USA: 2012. [Google Scholar] Cantonese, Nicole. "Could Red Wine Save Your Life?" Red Wine Effects. Refinery 29, 29 Mar. 2013. Web. 10 Feb. 2015. http://www.refinery29.com/red-wine

Lukas P. Inventing Wine: A New History of One of the World's Most Ancient Pleasures. WW Norton & Company; New York,

NY, USA: 2012. [Google Scholar]

Diaz, Jessica. "The Best Wines for Resveratrol." The Best Wines for Resveratrol. Livestrong.com, 16 Aug. 2013. Web. 2 Mar. 2015. <http://www.livestrong.com/article/150470-thebest-winesforresveratrol/>

Caviling G., Straniero S., Donati A., Begriming E. Resveratrol requires red wine polyphenols for optimum antioxidant activity. J. Nutr. Health Aging. 2016;20:540–545. doi: 10.1007/s12603-015-0611-z. [PubMed] [Crossruff] [Google Scholar]

Diaz, Jessica. "The Best Wines for Resveratrol." The Best Wines for Resveratrol. Livestrong.com, 16 Aug. 2013. Web. 2 Mar. 2015. <http://www.livestrong.com/article/150470-thebestwinesforresveratrol/>

Singleton V.L., Rossi J.A. Calorimetry of total phenolic with phosphomolybdic-phosphotungstic acid reagents. Am. J. Enol. Vitic. 1965;16:144–158. [Google Scholar]

Klutzy A.L. Alcohol and cardiovascular diseases. Expert Rev. Cardiovas. Thera. 2009;7:499–506. doi: 10.1586/erc.09.22. [PubMed] [Crossruff] [Google Scholar]

Cantonese, Nicole. "Could Red Wine Save Your Life?" Red Wine Effects. Refinery 29, 29 Mar. 2013. Web. 10 Feb. 2015. <http://www.refinery29.com/red-wine>.
https://www.arenaflowers.com/blogs/news/history-of-wine/
https://en.m.wikipedia.org/wiki/Wine
https://www.arenaflowers.com/blogs/news/history-of-wine/
https://www.arenaflowers.com/blogs/news/history-of-wine/
Garrett, Paul. "Red Wine Information and Basics." Basic Red Wine Knowledge. Wine Enthusiast. Web. 10 Feb. 2015. <http://www.winemag.com/red-winebasic
https://www.arenaflowers.com/blogs/news/history-of-wine/
https://www.arenaflowers.com/blogs/news/history-of-wine/

Garrett, Paul. "Red Wine Information and Basics." Basic Red Wine Knowledge. Wine Enthusiast. Web. 10 Feb. 2015.
http://www.winemag.com/red-winebasics/

Health Benefits of Wine." Polyphenols in Red Wine. French Scout, 1 Sept. 2010. Web. 10 Mar. 2015.
http://www.frenchscout.com/polyphenols

"Negative Effects of Vodka." Negative Effects of Vodka. Beverages and Health. Web. 2 Mar. 2015.<http://beveragesandhealth.com/negative-effects-ofvodka/>.

Postulate, Victoria. "The Benefits of Drinking Red Wine: How Red Wine Can Help Prevent Heart Disease." The Benefits of Drinking Red Wine. Hub pages, 25 Oct. 2014. Web. 10 Feb. 2015. http://vicky022389.hubpages.com/hub/Red-Wine-forYourHealth

."The Types of Red Wine." The 8 Major Types of Red Wine. French Scout, 1 Jan. 2012. Web. 2 Mar. 2015 <http://www.frenchscout.com/types-of-red-wines>.

www.ingramcontent.com/pod-product-compliance
Lightning Source LLC
LaVergne TN
LVHW091531070526
838199LV00001B/15